KEY TO
NATIVE TREES

START HERE

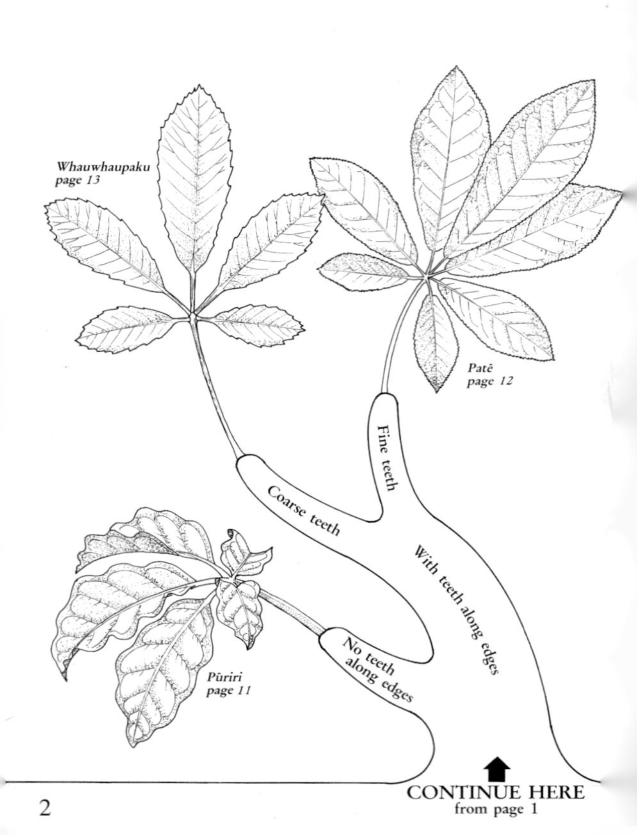
Whauwhaupaku
page 13
Patē
page 12
Fine teeth
Coarse teeth
With teeth along edges
Pūriri
page 11
No teeth
along edges
CONTINUE HERE
from page 1

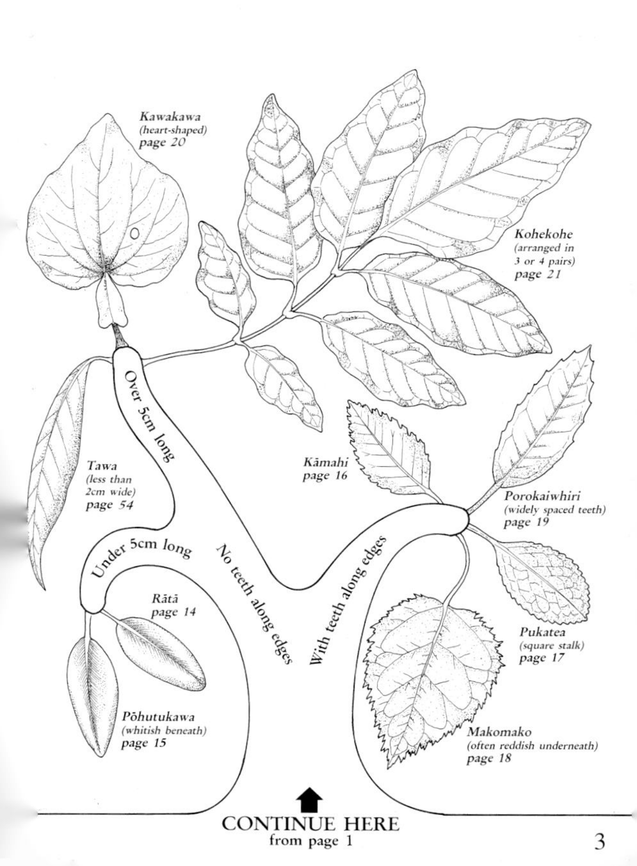

CONTINUE HERE
from page 1

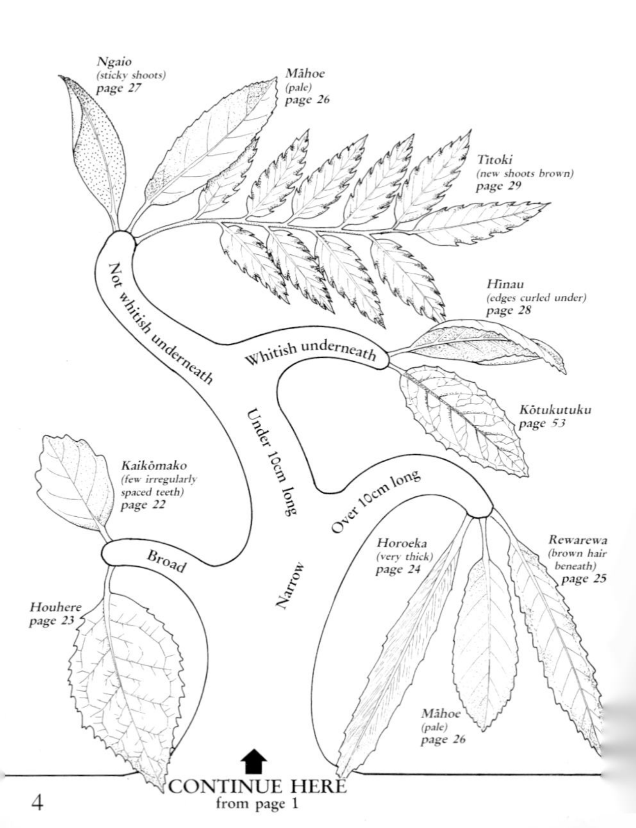
Ngaio
(sticky shoots)
page 27
Māhoe
(pale)
page 26
Titoki
(new shoots brown)
page 29
Hīnau
(edges curled under)
page 28
Not whitish underneath
Whitish underneath
Kōtukutuku
page 53
Under 10cm long
Over 10cm long
Kaikōmako
(few irregularly
spaced teeth)
page 22
Broad
Narrow
Horoeka
(very thick)
page 24
Rewarewa
(brown hair
beneath)
page 25
Houhere
page 23
Māhoe
(pale)
page 26
CONTINUE HERE
from page 1

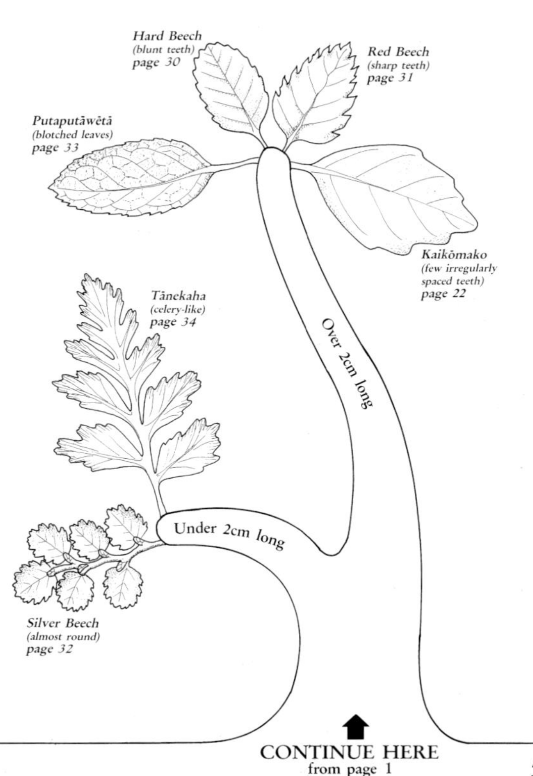

CONTINUE HERE
from page 1

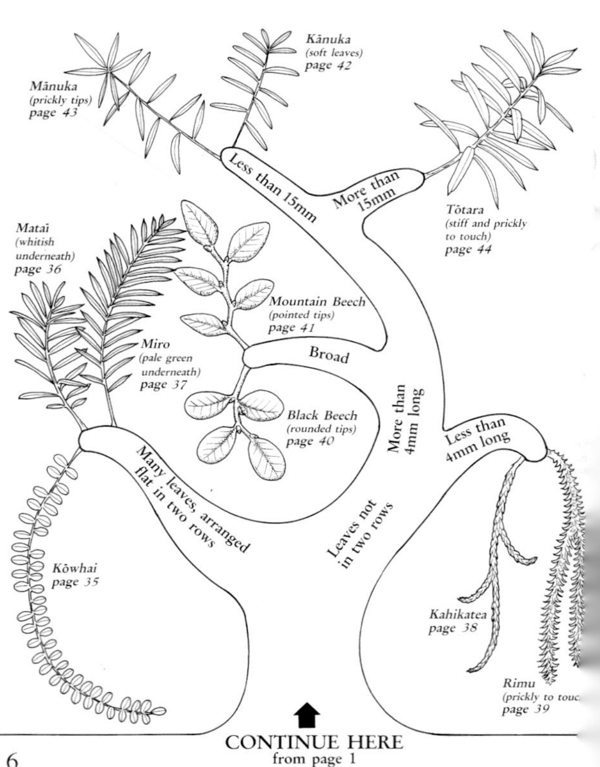

CONTINUE HERE
from page 1

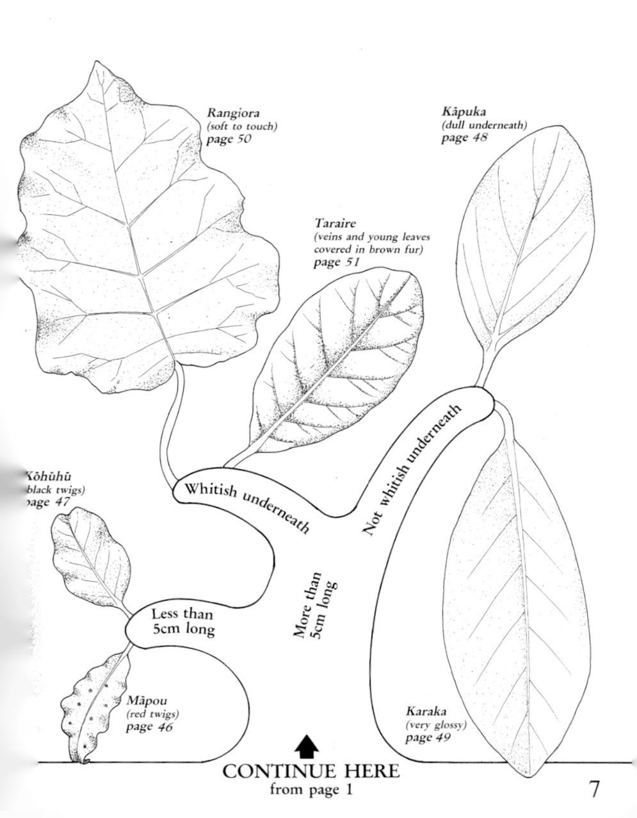

CONTINUE HERE
from page 1

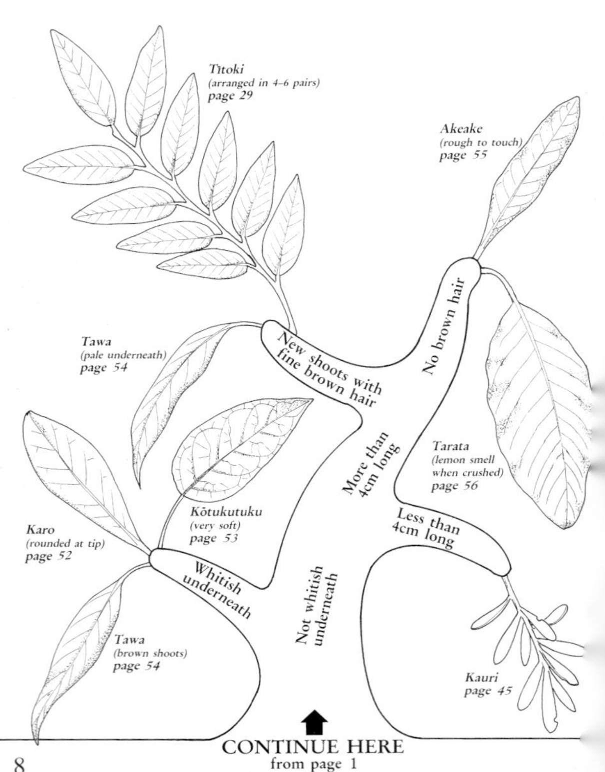

CONTINUE HERE
from page 1

Nīkau

Rhopalostylis sapida

Typical palm fronds, meeting to form a bulbous head.

Small, pink flowers, on long spreading fingers (late spring to early autumn).

Small, red fruit, in finger-like bunches (mostly late summer to early autumn).

Fronds were woven to make the roofs of dwellings.

Tī Kōuka/Cabbage Tree

Cordyline australis

Leaves 50 cm–1 m long, narrow, grass-like, growing in ball-like tufts.

White, sweet-scented flowers, tiny, but in large showy bunches (late spring).

Small, bluish-white fruit (late summer).

The heart of the tree has been cooked as cabbage.

Pūriri

Vitex lucens

Hand-shaped leaves, with 3–5 'fingers', no teeth, glossy, leaf stalks square-angled.

Pinkish-red flowers, 2.5 cm long (throughout the year but particularly in winter).

Round, red fruit, 2 cm across, look like cherries (throughout the year).

Fruit and flowers attract many forest birds.

Patē/Seven Finger

Schefflera digitata

Hand-shaped leaves, with 7–9 'fingers', fine teeth, thin, limp.

Small, greenish flowers, hanging in long fingers (late summer).

Very small, purple-black fruit, in long fingers on female trees only (autumn).

In spite of the name, does not always have seven 'fingers'!

Whauwhaupaku/Five Finger

Pseudopanax arboreus

Hand-shaped leaves, with 5–7 'fingers', large teeth, thick and leathery (unlike patē).

Tiny, sweet-scented flowers, in ball-like clusters (winter).

Tiny, black fruit, in ball-like clusters on female trees only (spring).

In spite of the name, does not always have five 'fingers'!

Rātā (Northern & Southern)

Northern *Metrosideros robusta*   Southern *Metrosideros umbellata*

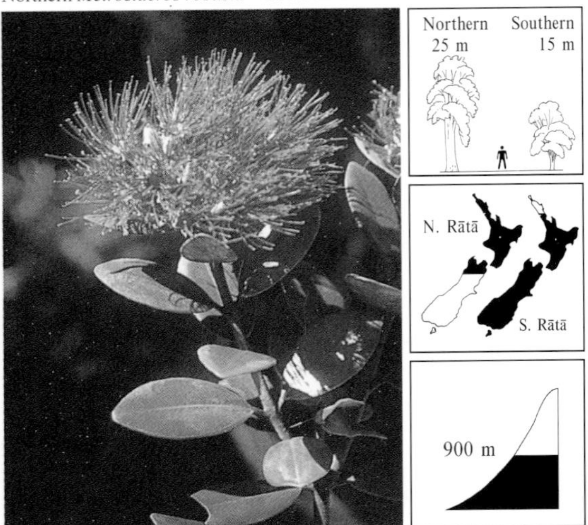

Opposite leaves, green (not white) beneath. (Leaf tips of southern rata are more pointed.)

Red flowers, in large spiky balls (summer).

Inconspicuous seed capsule.

Northern rātā often starts as a vine, later engulfing its host.

Pōhutukawa

Metrosideros excelsa

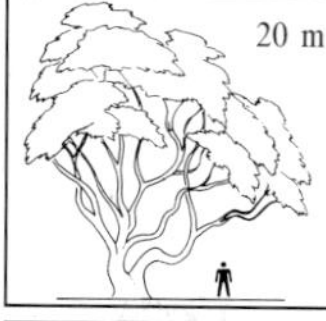

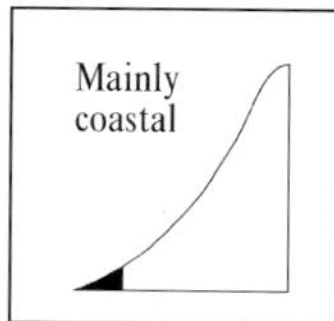

Opposite leaves, velvety white beneath, usually 5–8 cm long on white branchlets.

Red flowers, in large spiky balls (early summer).

Inconspicuous seed capsule.

These gnarled trees often noticed along northern cliffs.

Kāmahi

Weinmannia racemosa

Opposite leaves, 3–10 cm long (smaller and less leathery on juveniles), with large teeth.

Flowers almost white, fluffy, in finger-like clusters (late spring and early summer).

From afar, developing seeds can look like red flowers (summer to early autumn).

The northern variety of this is often called tōwai.

Pukatea

Laurelia novae-zelandiae

Opposite, dark, glossy, with rounded teeth, stalks square-angled, veins inconspicuous.

Flowers inconspicuous.

Seed cases green, jug-shaped (late summer), releasing fluffy seeds in autumn.

The trunk usually has plank-like buttresses at the base.

Makomako/Wineberry

Aristotelia serrata

Opposite leaves with deep teeth, usually reddish beneath, stalks red.

Small, pinkish-red flowers (late spring).

Small, dark red to black fruit (late summer).

The fruit was used by early settlers to make wine.

Porokaiwhiri/Pigeonwood

Hedycarya arborea

Opposite leaves, dark glossy green above, paler below, very widely spaced teeth.

Inconspicuous, but male flowers noticeably sweet-smelling (late spring).

Fruit in bunches, orange-red, on female trees only (late spring to early summer).

The New Zealand pigeon is attracted to the ripe fruit.

Kawakawa

Macropiper excelsum

Opposite leaves, heart-shaped, spicy smell when crushed, usually full of holes.

Inconspicuous flowers.

Yellow-orange fruit, usually 2–5 cm long on female trees only (mostly in summer).

Leaves chewed to alleviate toothache.

Kohekohe

Dysoxylum spectabile

Large leaflets in 3 or 4 opposite pairs, dark and shiny.

Long drooping sprays, white, sprouting directly from trunk or branches (early winter).

Round green capsule, 2.5 cm across, splitting to reveal orange-red centre (late autumn).

Dying out in many areas due to possum damage.

Kaikōmako

Pennantia corymbosa

Alternating or clustered, 3–10 cm long (less on young trees), irregular widely-spaced teeth.

Small, five-petalled, creamy white flowers, fragrant and profuse (early summer).

Small black fruit on female trees only (early autumn).

Name means food of the bellbird – they eat the fruit.

Houhere/Lacebark

Hoheria populnea

Alternating leaves, 5–12 cm long, large sharp teeth.

Large, white, star-like flowers (late summer and autumn).

Dry, winged seeds (winter).

Māori used the lacy inner bark for making headbands.

Horoeka/Lancewood

Pseudopanax crassifolius

Alternating, with teeth. On young trees 30 cm, on adults 7–20 cm, leaf rib and underside pale.

Inconspicuous flowers.

Small, purplish-black fruit, on female trees only (autumn and winter).

Very straight, lance-like trunk – hence the name.

Rewarewa/New Zealand Honeysuckle

Knightia excelsa

Long, stiff leaves with widely spaced teeth, midvein and new growth velvety brown.

In clusters, velvety, brick red in bud, peeling back to reveal yellow centres (late spring).

In long, rusty brown pods (summer).

A sweet nectar can be sucked from the tubular flowers.

Māhoe/Whiteywood

Melicytus ramiflorus

Alternating, with teeth. (After falling and rotting, these leave attractive leaf skeletons.)

Small, greenish-yellow, sweetly scented, growing on the bare branches (early summer).

Small, purple fruit, on female trees only (late summer).

Named for the smooth white lichen patches on the trunk.

Ngaio

Myoporum laetum

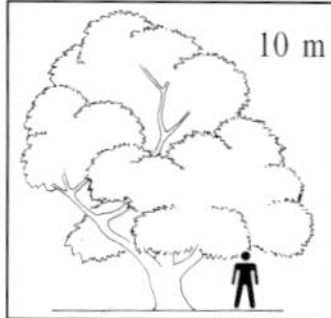

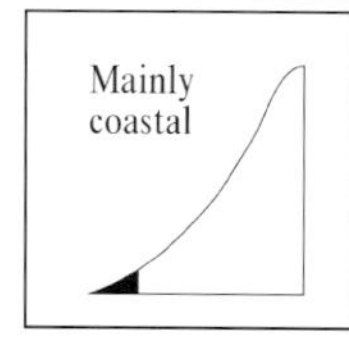

When held to the light, pale dot-like oil glands are visible, small teeth toward the tip.

Small, white flowers, with purple spots (late spring and early summer).

Small, reddish-purple fruit (early autumn).

Juice of sticky shoots deters mosquitoes and sandflies.

Hīnau

Elaeocarpus dentatus

Leaves 6–10 cm, whitish beneath, small bumps above, small teeth along curled edges.

Drooping flowers, bell-shaped, white (late spring).

Fruit purplish when ripe, 12 mm long (early autumn).

Māori used the flesh of the ripe berries to make cakes.

Tītoki

Alectryon excelsus

Alternating to near opposite, in 4–6 pairs, most without teeth, brown fur on new growth.

Inconspicuous flowers.

Hard, brown seed case, splits to show large shiny black seed in red pulp (early summer).

Oil squeezed from the seed was used by watchmakers.

Tawhai Raunui/Hard Beech

Nothofagus truncata

Alternating, 2.5–4 cm long, with blunt teeth, four or more veins on each side of central vein.

Male flowers tiny and red (spring). Female flowers inconspicuous.

Inconspicuous.

Silica in the timber makes it very hard to cut.

Tawhai Raunui/Red Beech

Nothofagus fusca

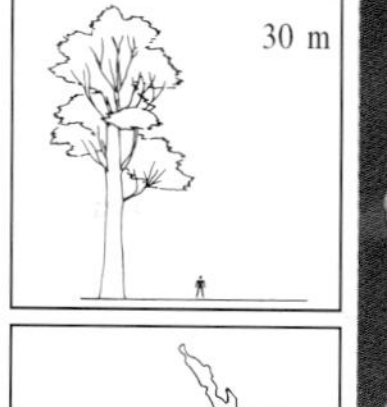

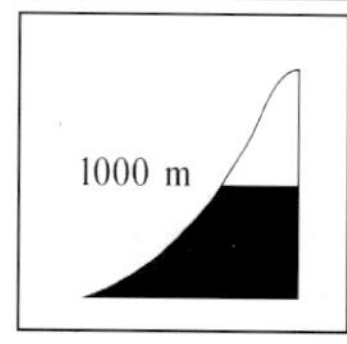

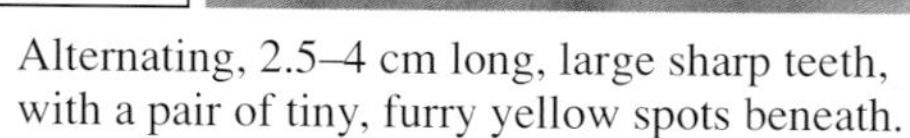

Alternating, 2.5–4 cm long, large sharp teeth, with a pair of tiny, furry yellow spots beneath.

Male flowers tiny and red (spring). Female flowers inconspicuous.

Inconspicuous.

The leaves of young trees turn red in winter.

Tawhai/Silver Beech

Nothofagus menziesii

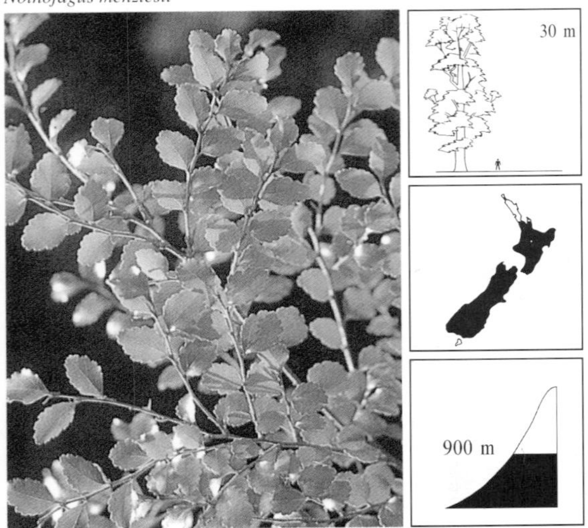

Roundish, 8–12 mm, with rounded double teeth; new shoots covered in brown fur.

Male flowers tiny and red (spring and early summer). Female flowers inconspicuous.

Inconspicuous.

Named from the silvery-white bark of younger trees.

Putaputāwētā/Marbleleaf

Carpodetus serratus

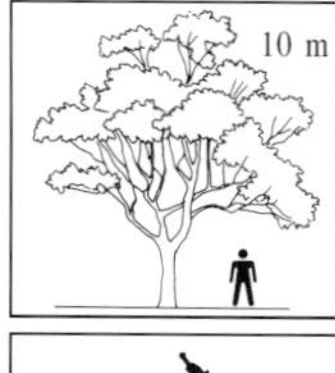

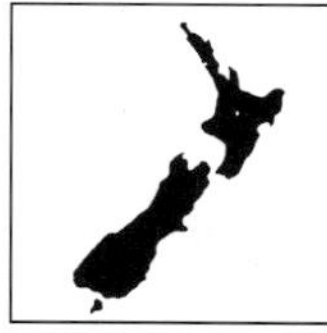

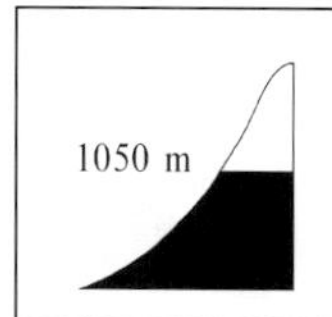

Small leaves with sharp teeth, and marble-like blotches (leaves of young trees, smaller).

Small, star-like flowers, white, in clusters, with a sweet scent (early summer).

Small, round, black capsule (early autumn).

Putaputāwētā means the trunk is 'full of wētā holes'.

Tānekaha/Celery Pine

Phyllocladus trichomanoides

Flattened leaf-like stems 1.5–2.5 cm long, fan-like and leathery, looking like a celery leaf.

The small male cones are red or purple (spring).

Inconspicuous.

The European name comes from its celery-like 'leaves'.

Kōwhai

Sophora microphylla

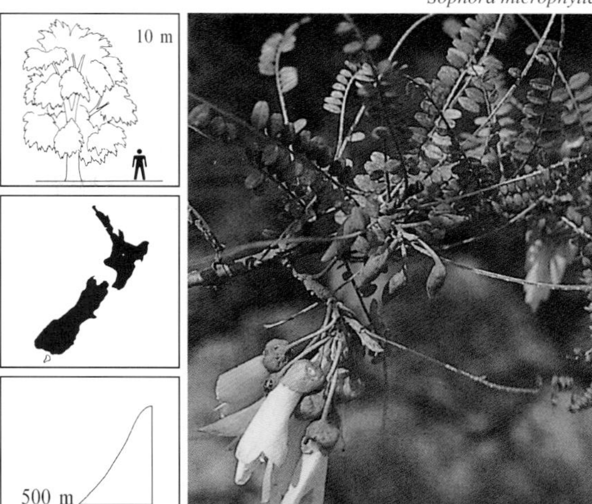

Small, rounded leaves, in many pairs, (losing most of its leaves in winter).

Large, bright yellow flowers, drooping, pea-like flowers (early spring).

Yellow bean-like seeds, in long, brown, hard, pea-like pods (winter).

Kōwhai is the Māori word for the colour yellow.

Mataī

Prumnopitys taxifolia

Leaves in two irregular rows, bluish-white beneath, with a strong smell when crushed.

Inconspicuous flowers.

Blue-black fruit, round, 1 cm across, on female trees only (summer).

Fruit popular with kererū (NZ pigeon) and kākā.

Miro

Prumnopitys ferruginea

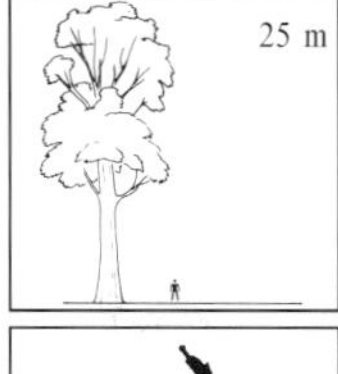

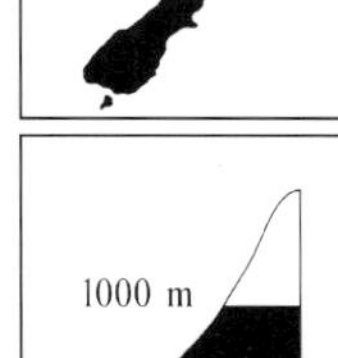

1000 m

In two neat rows, curved, pale green below, strong smell when crushed, over 1.5 cm long.

Inconspicuous flowers.

Pinkish-purple fruit, 2 cm long, on female trees only (all year).

Fruit a favourite of kererū (NZ pigeon) and kākā.

Kahikatea/White Pine

Dacrycarpus dacrydioides

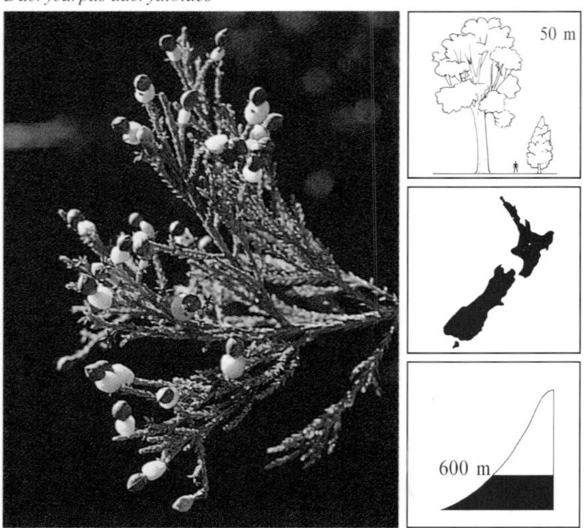

Tiny, scale-like leaves, overlapping (but in two neat rows on young growth), soft to touch.

Inconspicuous flowers.

Black seed on juicy orange-red base, on female trees only (autumn).

New Zealand's tallest and most ancient native tree.

Rimu

Dacrydium cupressinum

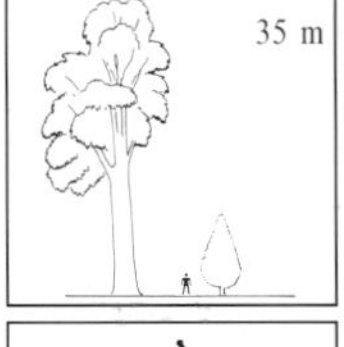

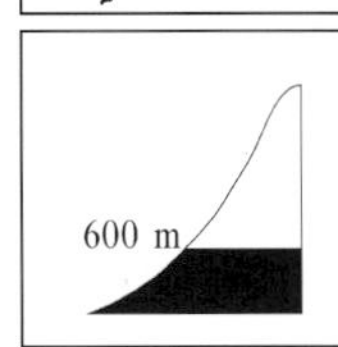

600 m

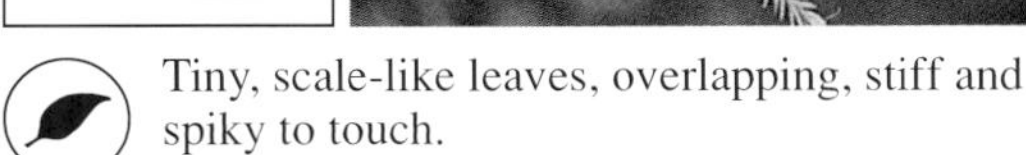

Tiny, scale-like leaves, overlapping, stiff and spiky to touch.

Inconspicuous flowers.

Black seed on juicy red base, on female trees only (mostly in autumn).

Previously an important building timber.

Tawhai Rauriki/Black Beech

Nothofagus solandri

Leaves have rounded tip, no teeth, 1–1.5 cm long.

Male flowers small yet of a striking red colour (spring). Female flowers inconspicuous.

Inconspicuous.

Named for the black bark on older trees.

Tawhai Rauriki/Mountain Beech

Nothofagus solandri var. *cliffortioides*

Triangular, pointed leaves, edges curled under, no teeth, about 1 cm long.

Male flowers tiny and red (late spring and early summer). Female flowers inconspicuous.

Inconspicuous.

Common in the mountains but found at sea-level too.

Kānuka/White Tea Tree

Kunzea ericoides

Leaves about 1 cm long, soft to touch, no spiky tip – unlike mānuka.

Profuse, very fragrant, white, in clusters, less than 6 mm across – unlike mānuka (summer).

Narrower, longer seed capsules than on mānuka.

Grows taller than mānuka. Leaves can be used for tea.

Mānuka/Tea Tree

Leptospermum scoparium

Leaves about 1 cm long, stiff, tip spiky to touch – unlike kānuka.

Usually white (sometimes pink), more than 6 mm across (most prolific in spring).

Hard, broad seed capsules – unlike kānuka.

Captain Cook and his crew made tea and beer from this.

Tōtara

Podocarpus totara

Very stiff leaves, spiky to touch, not in two rows, up to 2.5 cm long (longer on seedlings).

Inconspicuous flowers.

Green seed on juicy red base, on female trees only (in autumn).

The stringy bark was used as a splint for broken bones.

Kauri

Agathis australis

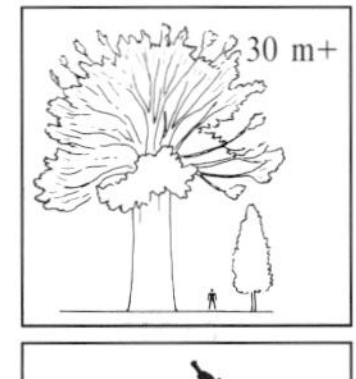

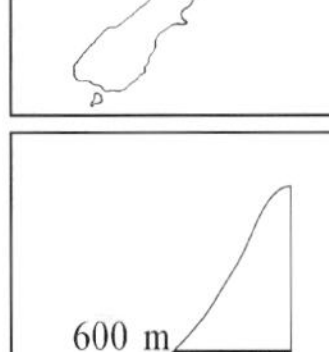

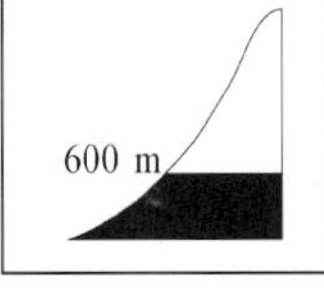

Leaves alternating to almost opposite, mostly 2–4 cm long (longer on young trees).

Inconspicuous flowers.

Female cones large and round. Male cones finger-shaped (spring and summer).

Some were believed to have been over 2,000 years old.

Māpou

Myrsine australis

Wavy edges, reddish green on new growth, often with reddish spots. Young stalks red.

Inconspicuous flowers.

Very small fruit, almost black, borne along the stalks (summer).

But for the red stalks, is easily confused with kōhūhū.

Kōhūhū

Pittosporum tenuifolium

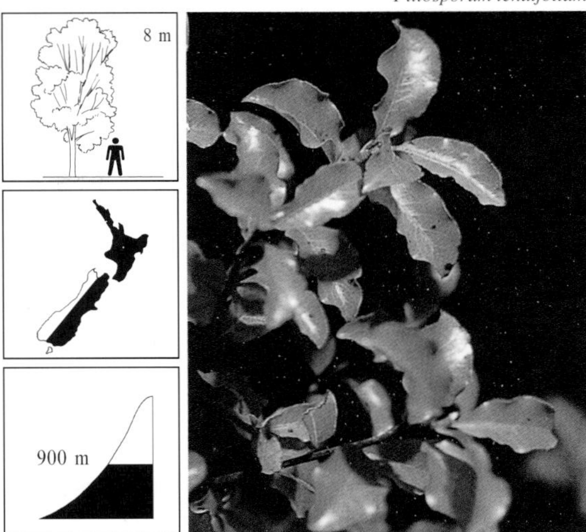

Leaves 3–6 cm long on blackish stalks, sweet smell when crushed, often with wavy edges.

Small flowers, very dark red to almost black, sweet-smelling at night (late spring).

Round dark seed capsule, splits to reveal sticky black seeds (ripe late autumn).

One of the *Pittosporum* scent plants of the early Māori.

Kāpuka/Broadleaf

Griselinia littoralis

Leaves often slightly unequal at base, dark green on top, never shiny below.

Inconspicuous flowers.

Very small fruit, purple-black, on female trees only (autumn).

A very hardy and popular hedge plant.

Karaka

Corynocarpus laevigatus

Dark leaves, glossy above and below, edges tightly curled under, 10–15 cm long.

Inconspicuous flowers.

Fruit orange when ripe, 2.5–4 cm long (summer).

The raw kernels of the fruit are VERY POISONOUS.

Rangiora

Brachyglottis repanda

Very large and soft leaves, mostly 10–20 cm long, white beneath, on long white leaf stalks.

Creamy white flowers, small but in large bunches, sweet smelling (spring).

Inconspicuous fluffy seeds.

Undersides of the large leaves make great notepaper.

Taraire

Beilschmiedia tarairi

Leathery, usually whitish beneath, mostly 7–14 cm, new growth with fine brown fur.

Inconspicuous flowers.

Large fruit, 3.5 cm long, dark purple (autumn).

Large fruit popular with kererū (New Zealand pigeon).

Karo

Pittosporum crassifolium

Alternating leaves, whitish beneath, 4–7 cm long.

Red to purple, about 1 cm across, heavily scented in the evening (mainly early spring).

Round and green, about 2 cm across, later bursting to reveal sticky black seeds (autumn).

Often growing with pōhutukawa and confused with it.

Kōtukutuku/Tree Fuchsia

Fuchsia excorticata

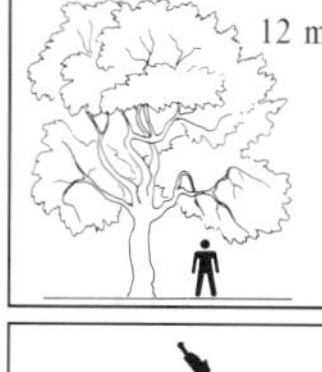

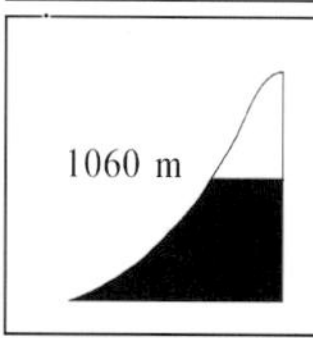

1060 m

Few or no teeth, white beneath with furry veins, soft. Can lose its leaves in winter.

Dark purple flowers, hanging, like garden fuchsia (late spring).

Fruit dark purple to almost black, narrow and about 1 cm long (summer).

The largest *Fuchsia* in the world. Loose, papery bark.

Tawa

Beilschmiedia tawa

6–10 cm long, pale beneath, hanging, graceful, willow-like, brown fur on new growth.

Inconspicuous flowers.

Fruit dark purple to black, 2–3 cm long (late summer).

Fruit popular with kererū (New Zealand pigeon).

Akeake

Dodonaea viscosa

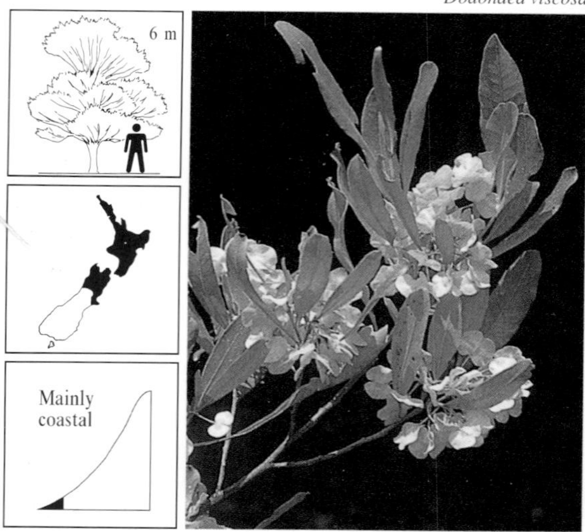

Sandpapery to touch, no teeth, 4–7 cm long, sometimes reddish. Leaf buds slightly sticky.

Inconspicuous flowers.

Hop-like seed capsules 1.5 cm across with 2–3 wings, on female trees only (summer).

The timber is hard, formerly used for mauls and clubs.

Tarata/Lemonwood

Pittosporum eugenioides

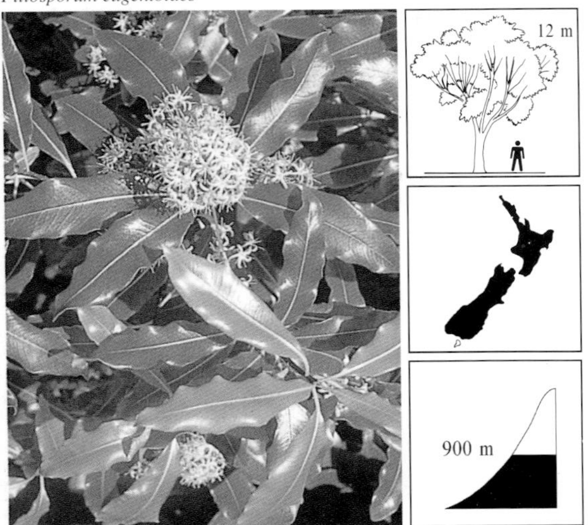

Scented when crushed, 7–15 cm, very glossy on top, edges wavy, midvein and stalk pale.

Starry, cream flowers, in bunches, sweet-smelling (late spring).

Round, dark seed capsule splits to reveal sticky black seeds (ripe summer).

The lemony leaves were used by Māori as perfume.